Child's Dreaming

Poetry by
Kevin Gilbert

Photography by
Eleanor Williams

HYLAND HOUSE

To all children everywhere and with special thanks to all
the little animals and other life forms who have given
generously of their beauty to this book.

First published in 1992 by
Hyland House Publishing Pty Limited
(ACN 005 268 208)
10 Hyland Street
South Yarra
Victoria 3141

This project was assisted by the Australia Council,
the Federal Government's arts funding and advisory body.

Australia Council
for the Arts

National Library of Australia
Cataloguing-in-publication data:

Gilbert, Kevin, 1933–

  Child's dreaming: poems.

  ISBN 0 947062 97 1.

  1. Children's poetry, Australian. I. Title.

A821.3

Typeset by Butler Graphics Pty Ltd, Hawthorn 3122
Printed in Singapore by Island Graphics Pty Limited

Contents

Hear the lilt of laughter

Hear the lilt of laughter
of the children while in school
they are tracking platypus
down by the swimming pool.
The children saw Mum Turtle's tracks
that led them to her eggs
a little further on they found
Blue Tongue who has short legs.
As they studied further
looking at the trees they saw
the scratch tracks made by Willai Possum's
sharp and shiny claw.
They saw where old Crow had his lunch
of some old piece of meat
and running tracks of Marsupial Mouse
that Dingo tried to eat
and then on the horizon
they saw a rainbow gleam
and listened to the legend
of what made Rainbow glow and beam.
After lunch they learnt to read
the message of the Birds
and what the Wind was saying
things you've never ever heard.

They read the dancing of the Ants
the flight of Native Bees
and what the Clouds were saying
high above the tall Gumtrees.
The children found some vegetables —
Yam and Cabbage Tree —
they must collect some fruit and meat
and then go home to tea.
They'd had a very busy day
and learnt a lot as well
they had a corroboree dance that night
with happy tales to tell.

Emu and Koori

When Captain Cook wrote his seafaring book
how could he have been so silly
to think he discovered Australia
before Emu and the Koori.

Little Pawprint

Here's someone's little pawprints
whose I do not know
carved upon the desert sand
in lovely sculptured row.
And is that hole an ant-lion's nest
or some small dry desert beast
that Little Pawprint's tried to find
to make a dinner feast.

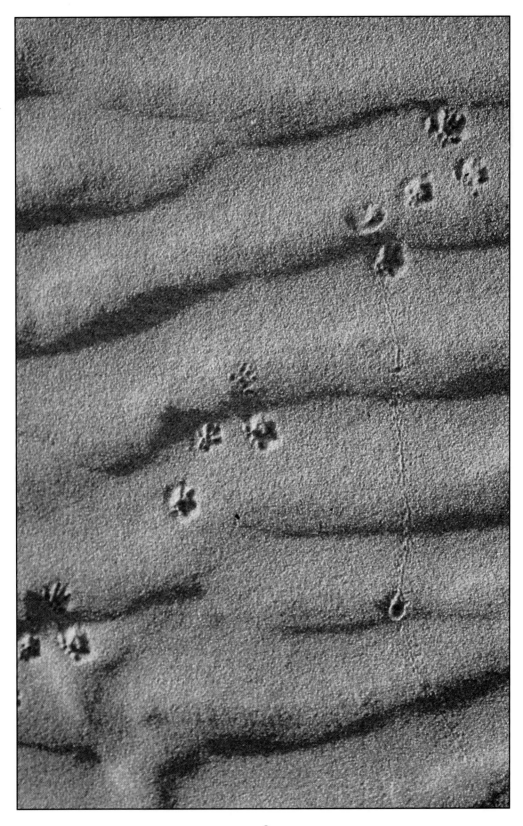

Turtle

Turtle likes to travel far
his home upon his back —
much better than a caravan
or a holidaying shack.

Eagle

I saw big Eagle watching me
while he sat on the old gum tree.
I thought, I'm glad I'm as big as me
and not as big as Finch.

The Weevil and the Beetle

Have you ever watched the Weevil
and the Beetle on the grass
they're so courteous to each other
and they each bow as they pass?

'Good Morning, Mr Weevil,
may I cross your territory?'
'With pleasure, Mr Beetle,
you're such pleasant company.'

Desert Pea

I stared hard at the Desert Pea
it had two eyes it was plain to see
I blinked and winked then stared again
but it didn't blink back at me.

Blue Tongue

Blue Tongue licked his lips today
I sat and wondered why
Mrs Mozzy shed a tear
and so did Mrs Fly.
Their juniors wouldn't listen
to what their mothers said
now Blue Tongue, nodding wisely,
looks contented and well fed.

Little Lizard

Little Lizard on the rock
doesn't go to school
he cannot draw or read or write
but he is no one's fool.
He knows it's warmer on the rock
when the south winds are chill
and where to go for dinner
so he can eat his fill.

Trees

Will you please stop
and look at me
an old and gnarled and friendly tree
and in your own imagery
look back through time
so that you see
the thousand birds who come to me
and rest their tired wings and sing
their lovely songs and poems and bring
their baby nestlings to my buds
and shelter them from storms' loud thuds.

If you should hear steel axes ring
or see a child do hurtful things
to trees like me, then please oh please
I'm your friend — the tree —
and save me, friend, so I may grow
stronger still and surely throw
you leaves and limbs to make warm fires
and stretch my beauty like tall spires
to shade and shelter you and be
a complete part of you and me
and Mother Earth.

Child's Dreaming

Within our hands
caress enfold as dreamings flow
to love and teach and guide
the soul and heart
in all the sacred things
that we hold dear
and wisdom in our heritage impart.

Spider

I'm a little spider
merrily I spin
my silver threads
to make a web
for the house that I live in
my pretty circle patterns
sometimes agleam with dew
so please don't break my nice house down
and I will spin for you.

Trapdoor Spider

Old Trapdoor often thinks it best
to close the trapdoor on his nest
he's such a nasty bitey thing
the Ant tribe would all come to fling
great ant-sized boulders down on him
if he didn't have a door.

Termites

The little termites build their house
with all their might and main
to store their food in summer
and keep out the winter rain.

They built them facing north and south
to keep them cool in summer
and protect them from the fires and flood
and porcupine Purra-Porra.

Purra-Porra Porcupine

I'm Purra-Porra Porcupine
you're sure to find my tracks
where I've been digging Ants' nests
to feast on Ants who lack
the sense to live in tree tops
or build their nests in logs
and my fine quills are
'cure them' pills
for Dingo and Sheep-dogs.

Desert Orange

The Desert Orange is hard to find
and it's harder to climb the tree
the fruit is good
its skin is green
and full of vitamin C.

Mopoke

Moock — poock
Mopoke

Sometimes it isn't a joke
when I fly at night
I feel a fright
from the floating creeping
ghostly shapes that walk
near the side of the swamp
and speak to me.

Moock — poock
Mopoke
at night it isn't a joke.

Wood Spider

I am wood spider, I have eight eyes it's true,
one to look at Magpie and one for Kangaroo
one for Jirri-Jirri, Giraw and old Emu,
two for Mopoke in the night and
one to wink at you.

Jirri-Jirri — Willie Wagtail
Giraw — Goanna

Brolga and Black Swan

The Brolga danced
upon the shore
before the huge Black Swan
it cried aloud:
'A mortal shroud
the feathers you have on.
Why don't you change your feathers
be white and nice like me
together we will dance and sing
such lovely company.'

The Black Swan curved a curtsy
thanked Brolga for the thought
and stated very firmly:
'We are as Nature wrought
both different and both beautiful
each a delight to see
come dance with joy and we will share
each other's harmony.'

Black Currawong

So you think you know
who I am
how clever my disguise
I'm not old Crow
I'm Black Currawong
look closely at my eyes!

I'll share a secret with you
(I know you'll keep it true)
old Crow's fierce eye
glints shiny blue
while mine are yellow hue.

Cicada

I'm a Cicada
I can sing
the same old thing
the same old thing
I am a Cicada
I can sing
the same old thing
the same old thing
all day.

Crab

I bet you can't guess who I am
my paws tucked under me
you're right — they're claws
and I am Crab
just resting after tea!

Whoo-hoo

There's too much to do whoo-hoo
there's too much to do whoo-hoo
so I sit in the tree
feeling sorry for me
when it's so much more fun
when the jolly thing's done
it's so much more fun whoo-hoo.

Pelican Chick

Here where the Pelicans build their nest
here where the sun shines red
they laid an egg for a Pelican chick
and they named that slick chick Zed.

Hairy Caterpillar

I'm a hairy Caterpillar
I sometimes live in clumps
with many legs and blotchy spots
and lots and lots of humps
I make myself a neat cocoon
and in silk sheets I lie
when the time is ripe and ready
I become a Butterfly.

Little Butterfly

Sleep little Butterfly
sleep in your cocoon
when you emerge tomorrow
you'll fly away so soon.

Shake your wings and spread them
hold them proud and high
let your colours sparkle
with sunbeams as you fly.

Letter-Winged Kite

The red desert Letter-Winged Kite
posed for his photo quite right
so that you may see
how handsome is he
at rest as well as mid-flight.

Kangaroo

You've heard of my son Joey
well I am Joey's dad.
Some cruel people try to shoot me
that's why I look so sad.

Wallabies

Wallabies like me
cannot ski
or go for a toboggan ride.
We get cold feet
from the snow
and the sleet
so we find a rock cave
and we hide.

Guddi Guddi Black Snake

Guddi Guddi old black snake
look at the squiggly tracks you make
stay in the sun and do not flee
I won't come any closer — oh no not me.

Children Dancing

Children dancing holding hands
dancing the stories of our peoples' land
painting our bodies with the ochre and clay
boomerangs clapping in the proper way
digging the yam song, cockatoo,
emu-man and crocodile and kangaroo.

winnowing, winnowing, winnowing,
winnowing the seed,
winnowing, digging, digging yams and
winnowing the seed.

Children dancing holding hands
dancing the stories of our peoples' land
boys dance hunting dance and jabiru
girls dance winnowing and cockatoo.

Children dancing holding hands
dancing the stories of our peoples' land
body paints and feathers are gleaming
   bright
little feet are pounding on the earth and
   sand.

Children dancing holding hands
dancing the stories of our peoples' land
painting our bodies with the ochre and clay
boomerangs clapping in the proper way
digging the yam song, cockatoo
emu-man and crocodile and kangaroo.

winnowing, winnowing, winnowing,
winnowing the seed,
winnowing, winnowing, winnowing,
winnowing the seed.

Our Sacred Family

I'm a part of every living thing
and every living thing is part of me.
We're all created of this sacred earth
so everything's our sacred family.

e